THE SILENT SECOND

THE BIOGRAPHY OF MARTIN CAPAGES CAPTAIN-USMC

By Martin Capages Jr. PhD

© 2018 Martin Capages, Jr.

All rights reserved. No part of this book may be reproduced or utilized in any form or by any means, electronic or mechanical, including photocopying, recording or by any information storage retrieval system without permission in writing from the publisher, except for a reviewer who may quote brief passages in a review to be printed in a newspaper, magazine or electronic publication.

American Freedom Publications LLC
www.americanfreedompublications.com
2638 E. Wildwood Road
Springfield, Missouri 65804

ISBN 978-1-64440-379-2   Paperback Version

Cover Design   Christopher. M. Capages
www.capagescreative.com

Manuscript Editor   Karissa Elaine McCarter

First Edition- 10 November 2018

Printed in the United States of America

MILITARY CODE OF CONDUCT

I am an American fighting in the forces that guard my country and our way of life, I am prepared to give my life in their defense.

I will never surrender of my own free will. If in command, I will never surrender the members of my command while they still have the means to resist.

If I am captured, I will continue to resist by all means available. I will make every effort to escape and aid others to escape. I will accept neither parole nor special favors from the enemy.

If I become a prisoner of war, I will keep faith with my fellow prisoners. I will give no information nor take part in any action which might be harmful to my comrades.

If I am senior, I will take command. If not, I will obey the lawful orders of those appointed over me and will back them up in every way.

Should I become a prisoner of war, I am required to give name, rank, service number, and date of birth. I will evade answering further questions to the utmost of my ability. I will make no oral or written statements disloyal to my country and its allies.

I will never forget that I am an American fighting for freedom, responsible for my actions, and dedicated to the principles which made my country free.

I will trust in my God and in the United States of America.

THE SILENT SECOND

DEDICATION

Martin Capages
Captain-USMC

THE SILENT SECOND

ACKNOWLEDGEMENTS

Photo Credits:

Public Domain:

https://www.archives.gov/research/military/ww2/photos

With permission:

https://www.worldwarphotos.info

Photo of Colonel Yahara, Courtesy John Wiley & Sons Inc.

THE SILENT SECOND

TABLE OF CONTENTS

MILITARY CODE OF CONDUCT iii
DEDICATION v
ACKNOWLEDGEMENTS vii
FOREWORD xi
PREFACE xv
INTRODUCTION 1
WWII NAVAL AND COAST GUARD SHIP DESIGNATIONS 8
MARTIN CAPAGES 270848 9
MARTIN CAPAGES 032320 15
INVASION PLANNING 19
PREPARING FOR OKINAWA 29
JAPANESE DEFENSE PLAN 39
SECOND DIVISION "DEMONSTRATION" 45
RETURN TO SAIPAN 61
POST WORLD WAR II 69
THE HOME FRONT 73
KOREA 77
PEACETIME 1953-56 85
MARINE CORPS PHOTOS 99
MARINE BRAT PHOTO ALBUM 101
EPILOGUE 105
POSTSCRIPT 107
ABOUT THE AUTHOR 109
WORKS CITED 111
INDEX 113

THE SILENT SECOND

FOREWORD

My friend, Martin Capages Jr. PhD, is a proud and confident man, a man of intelligence, energy and high standards. He is a thoughtful participant in the political dialogue that is one of the major "sports" among many educated people with conviction and passion. Dr. Capages has both the conviction and courage to take on the numerous left-leaning contributors to the local newspaper, the Springfield News-Leader. I have great respect and admiration for his willingness to defend traditions and standards of the Judeo-Christian society in which we were nurtured as boys.

Now, Dr. Capages has asked me to write the foreword to *The Silent Second*. Although I have never written a foreword, I welcome the opportunity to say something about the author, a true patriot and a man l greatly admire and respect. Therefore, as a fellow flag waver I would like to do him justice.

As I reviewed *The Silent Second*, the writer evoked memories of my own experiences as a Marine with a family. Like Martin's family, our family also traveled extensively, met the periodic challenges of making new friends, starting new schools and earning credibility on the job. Here, I would note and consider it significant that Martin's reflections are very positive. He seems always to recall the best in neighbors-adults and children, schoolmates and even the challenges his family faced from time to time. This positive attitude, in itself, tells me that the Capages family were all good Marines! Yes, I assure you that family members are often required to be as tough as their sponsors.

By discussing in considerable detail, Operation ICEBERG, (The 1945 Battle for Okinawa) and his father's role in the Western Pacific during the closing months of WWII and then addressing the Korean Conflict ('50-'53), the writer has set a time frame that nearly covers his father's Marine Corps service: Martin Capages Sr. enlisted in 1939 and left the Marine Corps in 1956.

Dr. Capages has titled this book, *The Silent Second*, but for me, his subtitle, *The Biography of Martin Capages, Captain USMC*, is a better clue to what lay ahead.

The writer's description of WWII and the amphibious operations in the Western Pacific, including Saipan, Tinian, as well as Okinawa, were informative. I had studied this in college but have now forgotten much of it. It is obvious that Martin Capages Sr. was often in harm's way at that time.

But whatever the personal risk may have been to Captain Capages in the waning days of WWII, his closest brush with death came some years later during the Korean Conflict when he contracted Korean Hemorrhagic Fever and was almost a victim of this ugly and painful killer.

My favorite part of Dr. Capages' writing is his perceptive coverage of the familiar: In the upbeat stories of people in his life, old and young alike, his use of Marine Corps jargon, Navy/Marine Corps terminology, and the mention of specific

Marine Corps places and activities brought back good memories. Perhaps he and I share a touch of nostalgia.

Bottom Line Impression: *The Silent Second* could be entitled *The Biography of Martin Capages, Captain USMC*. It is, as intended, very honoring to the man who gave this writer his name, his love and an enduring pride in this country. As a son of Greek immigrants, U. S. Marine Captain Martin Capages proved once again that the United States was and is the greatest country in the world. God bless the United States!

Semper Fi

Colonel Robert S. Coulter USMC

PREFACE

There are many veterans of World War II that kept their experiences to themselves. My dad was one of those. He never spoke of his time in battle or even the loss of his best friend at Iwo Jima. Any glimpses of these traumatic moments were relayed to me and my younger sisters by my mom. A career Marine, my dad was with the 2nd Marine Division at Okinawa in April 1945 and also served with the 1st Marine Division in 1951-52 where he nearly died in Korea from hemorrhagic fever. These were family secrets. We were always told that Dad was away on maneuvers. Marine brats are used to that. After all, my dad had no middle initial in his name. It was Martin Capages, first initial M., last initial C., or MC as in Marine Corps. I decided to research and perhaps document the experiences that my dad may have had as a Marine officer in the Second Division, the Silent Second and the First Division, The Old Breed. This led to the need to set the scene by telling some of the Capages family history. That may seem boring to some. My dad was unique. He was the smartest man I would ever know, an officer and a gentleman. The United States Marine Corps was his life until a Reduction in Force in 1956. At that time, Captain Capages was the Officer-in-Charge of the 6th Signal Company and the Marine Recruiting Station at Alameda, California.

Captain Capages discusses role of a Marine Signal Company with Miss Alameda in 1956

The Marines offered my dad a reduction in rank from Captain to Warrant Officer with the ability to retire after two years at the rank of Captain, having completed 20 years of service. Dad resigned after 18 years as a Marine. Sometimes the Marine brass forgets what Semper fidelis means during peacetime.

I appreciated the reminder on that very topic by General Wallace M. Greene Jr.-Commandant of the Marine Corps-in his Foreword to Victory and Occupation, History of the U. S. Marine Corps Operations, Volume V in 1968. That publication was the source of much of the operational information and planning for the invasion of Okinawa contained in this book. According to General Greene, "Like other active duty Marines at the end of the war, I, too, experienced the period of transition when the Corps reverted to a peacetime role in the defense of this nation. Responsive to its combat experiences in World War II, the Marine Corps made many tactical and organizational changes, as this book (Volume V) shows. Unchanged, however, was our highly prized esprit de corps, which, even as this is written, is being as jealously guarded as when our Corps was first formed." (Frank, 1968) But, this Marine brat is adding this personal note and, perhaps, a warning to future Commandants of the Marine Corps. Do not lapse into the behavior of a peacetime force. Respect and retain your base of experience while preparing for the next action, not the last war.

My earliest Marine brat memory is that of a four-year-old getting a small pox vaccination at the base dispensary at Camp Lejeune in 1948. The next stop was kindergarten at

PREFACE

Camp Pendleton followed by the first grade in Winthrop Harbor while my dad was assigned at the Great Lakes Naval Air Station. Then second grade in Millington, Tennessee where a Navy doctor at that Naval Air Station pulled out my tonsils. As I went under the ether he asked me, "are you going to be a sailor?" Of course, my response was, "No sir, I'm going to be a Marine." He promised me all the ice cream I could eat after the surgery. That didn't happen so, I never trusted the Navy after that. Then it was back to Camp Lejeune for a year then off to Alameda, California in the fall of 1954. There is the old saying that "if the Marines meant for you to have a family, they would have issued you one with your uniform." During my dad's service with the Marines, I would never attend the same school two years in a row. But, the Marine Corps would be kind to their Marine families as long as you stayed mobile. That was my experience anyway. If you are part of a Marine family, you can probably relate to the short family history that I have just described. If you're a civilian, perhaps you will now have a better understanding of the military and the sacrifices made to protect the Nation.

This is the story of career Marine, a proud member of the Second Marine Division during World War II who also served in the First Marine Division in Korea. It includes some detail on an important assignment successfully completed by the Silent Second in World War II with little fanfare. That was the initial intent of this biography which begins at the final stages of planning for Operation Iceberg, code name for the Battle for Okinawa. While there is an overwhelming amount of documentation on this battle, in particular, the role of the 1st and 6th Marine Divisions' and the Army's action at Okinawa, the Silent Second's role is a footnote in history. The 1st and 6th just walked ashore, meeting little resistance. That resistance would come later on, but initially it was a "cake walk." There was reason for this. To find out, just Follow Me.

Martin Capages Jr. PhD

INTRODUCTION

The combined assault and capture of Okinawa was the most ambitious joint Army-Navy-Marine Corps operation in the history of the Pacific War. Statistically, in comparison to previous assaults in this war zone, the numbers of men, ships, and planes as well as the tons of munitions and supplies employed in this campaign exceeded that of the 6 June 1944 D-day beach landings at Normandy.

The Okinawa landing was the culmination of amphibious warfare in the Pacific Theater of World War II. Amphibious operations are the specialty of the U. S. Marines and is their heritage; but, Operation Iceberg would be the most audacious and complex military effort undertaken by the amphibious forces of the Pacific Fleet. The landing operation at Okinawa also marked the last major ground action of the war against Japan. It provided insight into the sheer magnitude of the resistance the Japanese would muster in the defense of their homeland and the massive casualties that the invasion of Japan would cause on both sides. The forecast of estimated casualties, based on information yielded by the Battle at Okinawa, led to the decision to end the war with the first use of atomic weapons.

INTRODUCTION

The three-month-long battle of Okinawa covered a 700-mile arc from Formosa to Kyushu and involved a million combatants--Americans, Japanese, British, and native Okinawans. With a magnitude that rivaled the Normandy invasion the previous June, the battle of Okinawa was the biggest and costliest single operation of the Pacific War. During 82 days of combat, the battle would claim an average of 3,000 lives per day from the antagonists and the unfortunate noncombatants.

"Imperial Japan by spring 1945 has been characterized as a wounded wild animal, enraged, cornered, and desperate. Japanese leaders knew that Okinawa in U.S. hands would be transformed into a gigantic staging base 'the England of the Pacific'--for the ultimate invasion of the sacred homeland." (Alexander, n.d.) The Japanese were willing to sacrifice everything to avoid the unspeakable disgrace of unconditional surrender and a foreign occupation. Defeat would violate the Samurai code of Bushidō. Bushidō was used by the military to present war as purifying and death a duty. Bushidō would provide a spiritual shield to let soldiers fight to the end. It would be used to recruit and inspire the suicide missions of the Kamikaze pilots.

The invasion and capture of Okinawa would present the U.S. Navy with its greatest operational challenge of the Pacific War: protecting an enormous and vulnerable amphibious task force tethered to the beachhead against the suicidal attack of the Japanese kamikazes, both in the air and on the water, as well as banzai attacks on land. Okinawa would be the proof that U.S. amphibious power projection had truly come of age--that Americans in the Pacific Theater could plan and execute a massive assault against a large, heavily defended land-mass, integrate the tactical capabilities of all services, fend off every imaginable form of counterattack, and maintain operational momentum ashore.

Operation ICEBERG could not be conducted in a vacuum. Action preliminary to the invasion would begin at the same time that major campaigns in Iwo Jima and the Philippines were still being wrapped up, a reflection of the great expansion of American military power in the Pacific, yet a further strain on Allied resources.

But as expansive and dramatic as the Battle of Okinawa proved to be, both sides clearly saw the contest as a foretaste of even more desperate fighting to come with the inevitable invasion of the Japanese home islands. Okinawa's proximity to Japan--well within medium bomber and fighter escort range--and its militarily useful ports, airfields, anchorages, and training areas--made the skinny island an imperative objective for the Americans, eclipsing their earlier plans for the seizure of Formosa for that purpose.

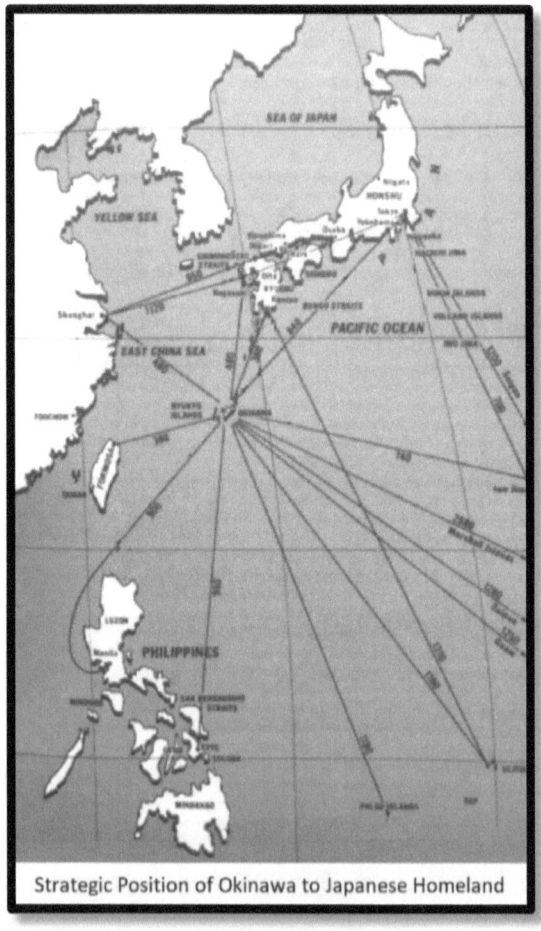

Strategic Position of Okinawa to Japanese Homeland

Okinawa, the largest of the Ryukyuan Islands, sits at the apex of a triangle almost equidistant to strategic areas. Kyushu is 350 miles to the north; Formosa 330 miles to the southwest; Shanghai 450 miles to the west. As with so many Pacific battlefields, Okinawa had a peaceful heritage.

Although officially one of the many administrative prefectures of Japan, and a Japanese territory since being forcibly seized in 1879, Okinawa prided itself on its distinctive differences, its long Chinese legacy and Malay influence and a unique sense of community.

The Japanese Imperial General Headquarters (IGHQ) in Tokyo did little to fortify or garrison Okinawa in the opening years of the Pacific War. Later on, after several strategic and tactical failures, IGHQ recognized the peril in which they had placed their homeland. On Okinawa, they established a new field army, the Thirty-second Army, and endeavored to funnel trained components to it from elsewhere. But American submarines would interfere with this and exacted a deadly toll. One U. S. submarine torpedoed a Japanese transport that caused the loss of 5,600 troops bound for Okinawa. It would take the Japanese the rest of the year to the replace that loss.

By October 1944 the U.S. Joint Chiefs of Staff (JCS) had recognized the paramount strategic value of the

Ryukyus and issued orders to Admiral Chester W. Nimitz, to seize Okinawa immediately after the Iwo Jima campaign. The JCS directed Nimitz to "seize, occupy, and defend Okinawa"--then transform the captured island into an advance staging base for the invasion of Japan.

In October 1944, Martin Capages was a second lieutenant in the Headquarters Battalion of the Second Marine Division. He had been training at Fort Sill, Oklahoma in the Communication course of the Field Artillery School. At that time, he was the Officer-in-Charge of the 1st Signal Company, Field Signal Battalion, Special Training Regiment at Camp Pendleton. He was then assigned as Company Commander of Radar Group B at Camp Pendleton and transferred to Fleet Marine Forces (FMF), Pacific in November 1944. He was headed to Saipan via Pearl Harbor.

The Second Marine Division would train at Saipan and conduct landing maneuvers at Tinian in preparation for their role at Okinawa. Their role would be a short one but successful by all accounts. They would suffer casualties along with their Navy, Army and Coast Guard comrades. The Second Division had been bloodied at Tarawa but were prepared to go all in, once again. They prepared for battle and trained on Saipan while mopping up the remnants of enemy resistance still on the island. The Division was a mix of combat veterans and new replacements, fresh from San Diego via Hawaii. The replacements celebrated Christmas 1944 in Hawaii with decorations on palm trees. They were a long way from home. Some would not see another Christmas. Iwo Jima and Okinawa lay ahead.

WWII NAVAL AND COAST GUARD SHIP DESIGNATIONS

SHIPS

    AH: hospital ship

    AKA: attack cargo ship

    AP: auxiliary transport

    APA: attack transport

    APD: high-speed transport

    LHA: amphibious assault ship

    LKA: amphibious cargo ship

    LPD: amphibious assault transport dock

    LSD: dock landing ship

    LSM: medium landing ship

    LST: Landing ship-tank

LANDING CRAFT

    LCI: landing craft, infantry

    LCM: landing craft, mechanized ("Mike boat")

    LCVP: landing craft, vehicle, personnel ("Higgins boat")

LANDING VEHICLES

    AAV: assault amphibian vehicle

    DUKW: amphibious truck

    LVT: landing vehicle, tracked ("amtrac")

    LVT-A: armored amphibian vehicle

MARTIN CAPAGES 270848

Martin Capages was born near Hell's Kitchen in New York City in 1919, the son of Greek immigrants who essentially escaped from the Turks in Smyrna, Greece around 1906. My dad was the oldest child with three younger sisters.

In those days, the local YMCA was a second home. Dad always thought the Greeks had the edge in weightlifting and body building. He would win some athletic competitions and would inspire one of his nephews to compete in this sport. The nephew's name was Jeff Smith, Mr. California 1973. Jeff's work-out partner was Arnold Schwarzenegger.

In high school, my dad developed an avid interest in science and mathematics. The fairly new technology of radio communications intrigued him. An avid hobbyist, he experimented with crystal radios in his high school science class and at home. Many kids did that in those days. He would tell me the story of his experiment at home with a crystal radio and a dry cell battery. In the experiment, he tuned the radio to a local broadcast and applied the battery across the crystal. There was a sudden amplification of the sound from the earphone. He told his high school teacher about it the next day. The teacher told him "it was impossible". In 1948 Bell Labs' invention of the transistor and resulting patent proved otherwise.

Dad finished high school in three years and then fulfilled his dream, to be a United States Marine. He enlisted in 1939 at age 19.

Martin Capages in 1939
Enlisted in U. S. Marine Corps-Age 19

He loved music and became a Field Music Corporal then Field Music Sergeant stationed at the Marine Barracks on Parris Island. Off duty was spent working out in the gym and outside if the weather was agreeable. Of course, "Every

Marine is a Rifleman." So, there were many hours at the rifle range.

Corporal Martin Capages

That marvelous Marine uniform of the day was an eye catcher, especially to a beautiful, blonde-headed young lady from Tennessee, Helen Elizabeth Powell. The United States entry into the War was looming and Helen Powell had joined the War Department after graduating at the top of her class at Bolton High School near Millington, Tennessee.

Some of the entertainment before the War were the many parades and special events that had the Marine Corps bands and drill teams as the centerpieces. There was magic between the two of them. But then 7 December 1941 happened and the time for fanciful parades was over. The courtship continued, and they were married 7 November 1942 in a Marine ceremony which included the passage under the Marine sabers and cutting the wedding cake with my dad's saber. My dad had married into a large family. My mother was the youngest of 13 siblings of the rural Powell family in Millington Tennessee. That family had a heritage that dated back to the Revolutionary War. Apparently my great, great, great grandfather was a lieutenant in the Virginia Militia and served with Nathanael Greene and George Washington. During World War II, every male Powell of age would wear the uniform of the United States in its service.

Early married life would include a tragedy, the loss of their first child before his first breath was taken. My cousin, Peggy Ann Hall remembers that sad event in a letter she sent me in 2003: "Granny and Granddaddy Powell were living in Bolton at that time. I was living south of Kerrville before the Navy took our farm to extend the runway for jets. Uncle Marty was in the Marines and Aunt Helen had come home to have their first child. I remember getting up that morning and going to eat breakfast. They told me Helen (my favorite aunt) had had her baby and he had died. I started sobbing and don't know if I even ate breakfast. The family all gathered at the Powell home. The baby was dressed in a long white gown (if I remember right) and lay in a casket in the parlor of the big old white farmhouse. He looked like a beautiful baby doll although there was a blue bruised-looking place on one side of his face. Aunt Helen was lying in bed in the room across the hall. I remember fanning and fanning her with a piece of cardboard (the weather was hot) until she told my mother or my Aunt Mary Rose (Chumney) in that wonderful caring voice she had that I had fanned so hard my arms were about to drop off. They sent me out to play with the other kids. I was there when they asked your mother if she wanted to see the baby before they closed the casket. She said yes, and I think my Uncle Marvin brought the little casket across the hall and held it down so Helen could see the baby. She reached up, put her hand in the casket to touch him and started crying."

Peggy's letter continues, "Your father came in from the service on emergency leave. I don't remember if he got there in time for the funeral. I don't even remember if there was a funeral. Anyway, he was there, and all the kids fell in love with your dad. While the men sat around talking crops and politics, he pulled his shoes off and went barefooted with us. He said he had never gone barefoot or eaten ice cream before. He taught us to play soccer but, I never could get the hang of bouncing the ball off my head. Several years later, after he left the Marines, he taught me to shoot a BB gun. I had a huge crush on your dad and learned every single verse of the Marine Corps hymn." My cousin, Peggy Hall, passed away in 2015. She was a beloved teacher of the Native American children in Tahlequah, Oklahoma and an avid researcher on the life of William Shakespeare. My dad was instrumental in her decision to go to Oklahoma in 1961 and help the kids there. Now, back to the Silent Second and Sergeant Capages.

MARTIN CAPAGES 032320

Martin Capages had done well in training exercises and as an NCO, so he was selected to go to the Officers' Candidate School. He received his commission as a Second Lieutenant in the Marine Corps Reserve on 17 November 1943 and attended the 41st Reserve Officers' Class.

Officer Candidate Capages

In July 1940, the Marine Corps had less than 30,000 men in uniform. With the patriotic surge following entry into the War in December 1941, new warriors were lining up for the Services and the Marine Corps had no problem in retention or in new replacements. The problems were in the logistics and training. These would be overcome. By January 1945 the Corps had over 400,000 Marines in uniform, both men and women. This would exceed a half million by the end of the war.

Newly commissioned Marine 2nd Lieutenant Martin Capages would be assigned to the Army's Field Artillery School at Fort Sill, Oklahoma and would graduate 27 August 1944. The following day, Martin Capages Jr. was born at Fort Sill. (21 years later, Martin Capages Jr. would return to Fort Sill to attend the Army Reserve Officers Training course. Martin Sr. thought that was funny coincidence.)

2nd Lt. Capages, his wife Helen, and Martin Jr.

After Fort Sill, Lieutenant Capages would be transferred to Camp Pendleton and assigned as the Officer-in-Charge of the 1st Signal Company, Field Signal Battalion, Special Training Regiment. He would then be reclassified from Reserve officer to Marine Regular and assigned as Company Commander of Radar Group B at Camp Pendleton then transferred to Fleet Marine Forces, Pacific in November 1944. At that time, no Marine ground force was engaged in a major operation against the enemy. But that was going to change.

Because the Marines were amphibious by design, their primary role would be in the Pacific Theater. On 2 December 1944, Dad boarded the USS Republic in route to Pearl Harbor then Guam on board the USAT Cape Cleare. At Guam he boarded LST #781 headed for Saipan, arriving there on 14 January 1945. He was assigned to the Signal Company for the Headquarters Battalion of the 2nd Marine Division.

The 2nd Marine Division, commanded by Major General LeRoy P. Hunt, had returned to Saipan after completing the conquest of Tinian. There the division absorbed up to 8,000 replacements and endeavored to train for a frustratingly varied series of mission assignments as, in effect, a strategic reserve. The unit already possessed an invaluable lineage in the Pacific War--Guadalcanal, Tarawa, Saipan, and Tinian--and its mere presence in Ryukyus' waters would constitute a formidable "amphibious force-in-being" which would, theoretically, distract the Japanese on Okinawa. Yet the 2nd Marine Division would pay a disproportionate price for its bridesmaid's role in the upcoming campaign.

General Leroy P. Hunt

INVASION PLANNING

OPERATION ICEBERG

By October 1944 the U.S. Joint Chiefs of Staff had recognized the paramount strategic value of the Ryukyus and issued orders to Admiral Chester W. Nimitz, Commander-in-Chief, Pacific Fleet/Commander, Pacific Ocean Areas, to seize Okinawa immediately after the Iwo Jima campaign. The JCS directed Nimitz to "seize, occupy, and defend Okinawa"--then transform the captured island into an advance staging base for the invasion of Japan.

Admiral Chester Nimitz

Operation ICEBERG, code name for the invasion of Okinawa, was to be launched on 1 March 1945, L-day. This date had to be flexible, however, since it would be affected

INVASION PLANNING

by the : (1) Capture of Iwo Jima in time for the prompt release of fire support units and close air support squadrons required at Okinawa ; (2) Prompt release of supporting naval forces and assault shipping from the Luzon operation; and (3) Attainment of undisputed control of the sea and air in the target area in preliminary strikes against the Ryukyus, Formosa, and Japan.

Admiral Raymond Spruance

Nimitz turned once again to his most veteran commanders to execute the demanding mission. Admiral Raymond A. Spruance, victor of Midway, the Gilberts, Marshalls, Marianas, and the Battle of the Philippine Sea, would command the U.S. Fifth Fleet, arguably the most powerful armada of warships ever assembled.

THE SILENT SECOND

Vice Admiral Richmond Kelly Turner, gifted and irascible veteran of the Solomons and Central Pacific landings, would again command all amphibious forces under Spruance.

Admiral Richmond Turner

But Turner's military counterpart would no longer be the familiar old war-horse, Marine Lieutenant General Holland M. Smith. Iwo Jima had proven to be Howlin' Mad Smith's last fight. Now the expeditionary forces had grown to the size of a field army with 182,000 assault troops.

General Holland Smith

Army Lieutenant General Simon Bolivar Buckner, Jr., the son of a Confederate general who fought against U.S. Grant at Fort Donaldson in the American Civil War, would command the newly created U.S. Tenth Army.

General Simon B. Buckner

The Tenth Army would consist of an Army corps, a Marine amphibious corps and a large naval contingent. Overall command for the invasion would be by General Buckner. General Buckner believed that it was important for him to have a joint staff. He therefore requested Admiral Nimitz to authorize a Marine and naval augmentation of his staff. When this request was granted, approximately 30 Marine and 30 Navy officers, and enlisted assistants from each of these services, were assigned and integrated within the Tenth Army staff.

Admiral Turner was concerned that 1 March 1945 had been scheduled as L-Day, the assault on Okinawa. He feared that unfavorable weather conditions, which generally prevailed in March, might possibly affect the conduct of the landings and unduly prolong the unloading of supplies on exposed beaches. Available meteorological data justified this concern, for from October to March the Ryukyus experienced strong northerly winds with a mean velocity of 17-19 miles-per-hour as well as frequent gales.

A generally moderate wind, averaging 11 miles-per-hour, marked the beginning of a typical summer monsoon period and characterized the normal weather for Okinawa in early April. This would be more suitable for the invasion. In any case, Admiral Turner requested that the possibility of landings along the east coast be re-evaluated. At the same time, he suggested that the value of a feint landing be determined and, if valid, it should be incorporated into the plan finally adopted for ICEBERG. This suggestion by Admiral Turner would eventually be carried out by the 2nd Marine Division on L-day.

After a lengthy discussion of the problems inherent in the proposed plan, the conferees concluded that a landing on the western beaches on 1 March 1945 was fraught with considerable risk. The alternatives were either a 30-day delay of the operation or a landing on the southeast coast on the date originally scheduled for the assault. All other possible courses of action were re-examined, with the result that the Hagushi Beaches on the west side of the island were recommended again as the site for the landings, even with the risk involved. The proposed invasion plan was labeled Plan Fox. Final approval of Plan Fox was withheld by Admiral Turner because he retained doubts as to the practicality of landing and supporting the proposed assault force of four divisions over the Hagushi beachhead. In spite of the objections of Admiral Turner, the Plan Fox estimate was distributed on 5 November for further review. When that review was completed on 9 November 1944, it upheld the original contention that Hagushi held the only beaches in southern Okinawa adequate to receive four divisions abreast and, subsequently, to allow the necessary logistical support for the operation.

The plan of attack called for advance seizure of the Kerama Retto Islands off the southwest coast, several days of preliminary air and naval gunfire bombardment, then a massive four-division assault over the Hagushi Beaches (the Marines of IIIAC on the north, the soldiers of XXIV Corps on the south). Meanwhile, the 2nd Marine Division with a separate naval task unit would make a feint toward the Minatoga Beaches on Okinawa's southeast coast in the same manner as its successful amphibious feint off Tinian. Love-Day (selected from the existing phonetic alphabet in order to avoid planning confusion with "D-Day" being planned for Iwo Jima) would occur on 1 April 1945.

In the face of these convincing arguments, Admiral Turner accepted the plan with the proviso that both Kerama Retto and Keise Shima were to be captured prior to the main landing. This would prove to be a very wise recommendation. In the early planning for this initial action, the 2nd Division was slated for the job. However, this was changed to be the responsibility of the Army. The 2nd Division would standby as the floating Reserve after conducting two feint landings, one on L-day then again on L-day +1. With only minor exceptions, General Buckner concurred with these modifications, and the revised plan was forwarded to Admiral Turner on 11 November 1944. The original target date of 1 March was changed twice within the next month, first to 15 March and finally to 1 April 1945, L-day.

The headquarters of Major General Roy S. Geiger's III Amphibious Corps (IIIAC) was on Guadalcanal. General Geiger planned to employ the 1st and 6th Marine Divisions in the assault, with General del Valle's division on the right (south) flank. The choice of these two divisions was logical since they were both located in the Solomons at the time and there would be no problem in establishing liaison. The question then arose regarding what steps would be taken if the Japanese were encountered in strength as IIIAC advanced eastward across Okinawa. The military planners were fairly sure that an additional division would have to be inserted in the line before the east coast was reached. General Smith took this question up with the Tenth Army commander, who agreed that IIIAC would have first call on the 2nd Marine Division.

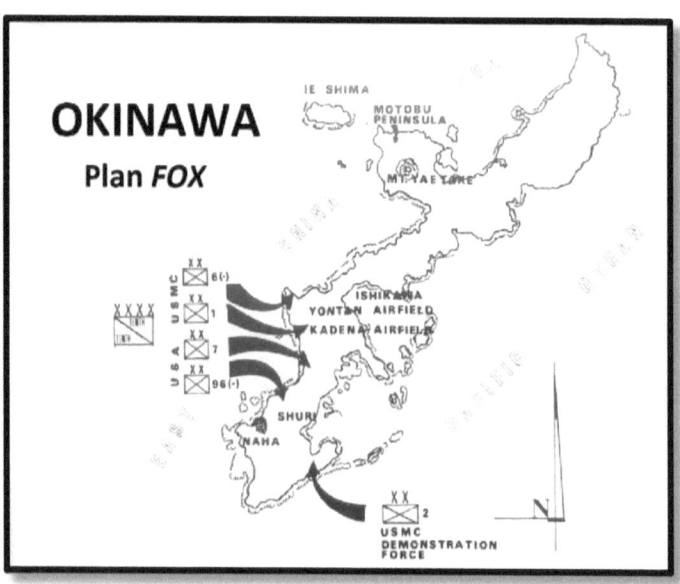

General Watson's division was scheduled to make the feint landings on the southeast coast of Okinawa on L-Day and L plus 1. The planners had not contemplated that General Geiger would need the 2nd Marine Division for actual land combat before the third day of the operation, if at all. That assumption proved to be correct. The plan was complete. It was now time to get ready.

PREPARING FOR OKINAWA

Fleet Marine Force ground training facilities by late 1944 had advanced far beyond those in existence at the beginning of the War. In addition to base command housekeeping and training units, Camp Lejeune had 10 battalions undergoing infantry training in January 1945 and Camp Pendleton had 12. Besides this number, Camp Pendleton housed four replacement drafts, a total of some 5,000 Marines, who were awaiting shipment to the Pacific. The training cadre of veterans were waiting for them on Saipan. Second Lieutenant Capages was one of those officers at the Battalion Headquarters.

Major General Lemuel C. Shepherd, Jr., based his 6th Marine Division at Guadalcanal, the same location as Geiger's IIIAC Headquarters. General Shepherd would go on to become the 20th Commandant of the Marine Corps.

General Lemuel Shepherd

The 1st Marine Division commanded by Major General Pedro A. del Valle was based on Pavuvu in the Russells, approximately 65 miles northwest of Guadalcanal. Major General Thomas E. Watson's 2nd Marine Division were based on Saipan.

General Pedro del Valle

General Thomas Watson

With the record number of six Marine divisions in the field, the constant demand for replacements and the heavy burden imposed upon the training command was nearly overwhelming. The Third Amphibious Corps (IIIAC) was made up of the 1st and 6th Marine Divisions with the 2nd Marine Division in reserve. The Fifth Amphibious Corps (VAC) was composed of the 3rd, 4th and 5th Marine Divisions. These three divisions were the amphibious landing force for the United States Fifth Fleet and were notably involved in the battles for Tarawa, Saipan, and Iwo Jima. The VAC was commanded by General Holland "Howlin Mad" Smith then followed by General Harry Schmidt. The VAC completed their training phases and began combat loading for the trip to the target areas, the anticipated demands for replacement of expected casualties on Iwo Jima and Okinawa were already being met by the organization and the training of new replacement drafts was underway.

As each Marine destined for assignment to a combat organization in the Pacific left the United States, he was aware that he was on the same path taken by fellow Marines who had fought at such now - famous places as Guadalcanal, Bougainville, and Tarawa. His sole consolation, if one was needed, was the knowledge that, although he had not participated in the beginning of the fight, he might possibly be there to help end it.

The veterans in the 2nd Division on Saipan and the 3rd Division on Guam, along with an increasing number of replacements participated in on-the-job training; mopping up survivors of the major Japanese defense garrisons which were defeated when those islands were officially declared secured in late 1944. On Saipan, more than 8,000 Marine replacements received this valuable on-the-job experience routing Japanese holdouts during the first months of the Division training program. Saipan's rapid build-up as a supply center and an air base restricted the training efforts of the division, however, and maneuver room and impact areas were soon at a premium. But there was some leisure time.

Sgt. John Powell 1945

John Powell and his father, Byron D. Powell

My uncle, John Powell was a sergeant in a quartermaster unit of the Tenth Army serving under Lieutenant General Simon B. Buckner. General Buckner was the overall commander of the land invasion of Okinawa. According to my dad, my uncle, nicknamed Big John (he was 6' 11" tall and 359 lbs.), paid a visit to his favorite bother-in-law on Saipan. Dad said, "I heard a sentry call out, 'Sir, there's an Army sergeant here who says you're his brother-in-law.' I could easily see who it was since he towered over the sentry. I said, 'Okay, let him in.' In comes Big John swinging both hands side by side, hiding a fifth of whiskey in the palm of each massive hand. Your Uncle John stood at attention, switched the bottle in his right hand to his left and holding both bottles in that massive left hand, he snapped me a salute with his right. Standing at attention, it was 'yes sir and no sir' for about two minutes then we both started laughing. It was a great reunion."

The Capages-Powell reunion wasn't the only relief from the insanity of war on Saipan. In the Heritage Years, R. L. Hofvendahl relates the story of The Easy Battery Barbeque on page 98. "It was February of 1945, the Saipan and Tinian operations were behind us and we were due to combat load in a couple of weeks for the next operation - Okinawa as it turned out, but we didn't know that then. I had been acting Battery Commander of E Battery, Second Battalion, 10th Marines, for two months. 'E Battery' became 'Easy Battery' in the military phonetic alphabet, and other than in written references I don't believe I ever heard it referred to other than as Easy Battery.... In November 1944 we had returned from Tinian, where we had been bivouacked since the island had been secured to Saipan, and where the rest of the Division was garrisoned. The Division had had a nine-month stay in New Zealand after

Guadalcanal, but that had been the last real taste of civilization and morale was low for the men. Gunnery Sergeant Walter White, one rank below First Sergeant, was our top-ranking nom-com. Despite our differences in background and outlook, we saw eye to eye on how to run this artillery battery. I heard him call out at the entrance to my pyramidal tent… 'Lieutenant, can I talk to you for a minute?' 'Come on in, Gunny, what's the problem? 'Those #%!! Battalion cooks are punching holes in the beer can issue when they pass it out!' I looked a bit puzzled, I'm sure. I knew that our people were getting a ration of two cans of beer a day and obviously they had to be opened sometime. 'Lieutenant, I'm really worried about some of these guys. They're beginning to look Asiatic as hell to me. You realize that it's been almost a year and a half since we shoved off from New Zealand. Most of them haven't even talked to a woman since then or gotten drunk or done anything.' 'What about Hawaii? His tone carried no resentment. 'That liberty wasn't too bad for officers and senior non-coms. It wasn't worth a, #%!! for most of the men - they didn't even leave camp. 'I'm beginning to see what you mean, Gunny.' I thought I really did see it clearly then, but I asked the question anyway. 'What's that got to do with the cooks punching out the beer when they issue it?' 'The men have to blow off some steam somehow. You don't get much mileage out of two cans of beer. If they want to save their ration and get smashed, I think they ought to be able to do it!'" That was the genesis of the Easy Battery barbeque which became, if not a legend in the Battalion, the most remembered garrison occasion in the history of Easy Battery. They saved their beer ration for a week, stole and butchered a steer from the indigenous people, found the perfect secluded place to unwind and the rest is history.

In the course of his inspection trip to Tenth Army units, General Buckner visited the 2nd Marine Division. On the morning of 3 February, he trooped the line of the 8th Marines and then inspected the regimental quarters and galleys. It seemed to General Smith that the men of the 2nd Division looked very fit and that they had made a tremendous impression on the Tenth Army commander. General Buckner was particularly impressed with the battalion commanders, and told his deputy chief of staff that "he had never before had the privilege of meeting such an alert group. . ." [Even if some of them may have had hangovers.]

A lack of suitable beaches on Saipan confined final division rehearsals to simulated landings only. On 8 March 1945, Dad boarded the attack transport, USS Sibley (APA-206), and left Saipan headed to Tinian in the Marianas and

PREPARING FOR OKINAWA

participated in amphibious maneuvers in preparation for the landings at Okinawa. Because of the indefinite nature of its employment once it had made the feint landings on L-Day and L plus 1, the 2nd Division had to select an arbitrary landing scheme of two RCTs abreast for the rehearsal pattern. Inclement weather prevented LVT launchings on two days, neither air nor naval gunfire support was available, and, finally, on 19 March—the last day of the exercises—only the naval portion of Task Group 51.2 (Demonstration Group) was able to participate in the Demonstration rehearsal. The maneuvers completed, Dad returned on the Sibley to Saipan and began organizing his Signal Company for combat operations. After a final rehearsal on the 24 March, he re-boarded the USS Sibley with his men and sailed for Okinawa on the morning of 27 March.

Marines boarding Attack Transport 27 March 1945

By the evening of 27 March, all other ICEBERG assault elements were at sea, converging on Okinawa. Soldiers and Marines aboard the transports and landing vessels had already made themselves as comfortable as possible under the crowded conditions and had settled down to shipboard routine. Officers and key NCOs reviewed their unit operation plans, examined maps and terrain models of the landing area, and held daily briefing sessions with their men. At the same time, they squared away their combat gear for the invasion. Most of the men of Hebrew and Christian faiths also prepared themselves for religious observances of Passover or Good Friday and Easter, all three holidays falling within a few days of each other., arriving there on 31 March. L-day, 1 April or Love Day was also April Fool's Day.

JAPANESE DEFENSE PLAN

The Japanese Imperial General Headquarters (IGHQ) in Tokyo did little to fortify or garrison Okinawa in the opening years of the Pacific War. With the American seizure of Saipan in mid-1944, however, IGHQ began dispatching reinforcements and fortification materials to critical areas within the "Inner Strategic Zone," including Iwo Jima, Peleliu, the Philippines, and Okinawa. (Alexander, n.d.)

On Okinawa, IGHQ established a new field army, the Thirty-second Army, and endeavored to funnel trained components to it from elsewhere along Japan's great armed perimeter in China, Manchuria, or the home islands. But American submarines exacted a deadly toll. On 29 June 1944, the USS Sturgeon torpedoed the transport Toyama Maru and sank her with the loss of 5,600 troops of the 44th Independent Mixed Brigade, bound for Okinawa. It would take the Japanese the balance of the year to find qualified replacements.

The Japanese Thirty-second Army staff planners wasted no time in organizing the ground defenses of Okinawa. They had learned by the cruel experiences of Japanese forces on islands which had been invaded by the Americans that a stand at the shoreline would only result in complete annihilation and that their beach positions would be torn to pieces in a naval bombardment. It became apparent, therefore, that the primary defensive positions had to be set up inland. Then, should the invaders escape destruction at sea under the guns and torpedoes of Japanese naval forces, or at the beachhead under the downpour of artillery shells, the death blow would be administered by the ground forces' assumption "of the offensive in due course." To steel the troops' determination to fight and to keep their morale at a high peak, army headquarters devised the following battle slogan:

-One Plane for One Warship

-One Boat for One Ship

-One Man for Ten of the Enemy or One Tank.

The command of the Thirty-second Army was assumed by Lieutenant General Mitsuru Ushijima in August 1944 with Major General Isamu Cho, as his chief of staff. On 21 January, army headquarters was split into two groups. Ushijima's operations staff moved to Shuri where the general was to direct his army for the major portion of the campaign. A "rear headquarters" composed of the ordnance, veterinary, judicial, intendance, and the greater part of the medical staff set up near Tsukasan, south of Shuri.

THE SILENT SECOND

Lieutenant Generals Ushijima and Cho complemented each other's military qualities and personality and formed a command team that reflected mutual trust and respect. They were ably abetted by Colonel Hiromichi Yahara, as Senior Officer in Charge of Operations, and Major Tadao Miyake as the logistics officer. Colonel Yahara, was senior staff officer of Japan's last fighting army, in charge of Operations-the rough equivalent of an American army G-3. A bright light of the Japanese General Staff, whose last post had been as an instructor at Japan's War College, Yahara became both the architect and executor of the entire Japanese defense effort in what would become the Pacific war's bloodiest military encounter, lasting from April to July 1945.

It was Yahara's concept of a yard-by-yard "war of attrition" (iikyusen) that made Okinawa such a hellish struggle. The purely defensive strategy was a complete departure from other Japanese island defenses, which had concentrated-with a notable lack of success-in attempts to "annihilate the enemy at the water's edge." By fighting for time, not victory, and doing so despite the obligatory grandiloquent sloganry of his communiqués to Tokyo, Yahara recognized far more clearly than his superiors in Tokyo the inevitability of final defeat. He would survive the war as a POW and document the battle in his book *The Battle for Okinawa* published by John Wiley and Sons, Inc. 1995.

Col. Hiromichi Yahara

General Ushijima was reputedly a man of great integrity and character who demonstrated a quiet competence which, in turn, inspired great confidence, loyalty, and respect from his subordinates. Cho, in comparison, was a fiery, ebullient, and hard-driving individual with a brilliant, inquiring mind. He spared neither himself nor his staff. His abounding energy was effectively counterbalanced by his senior's calm outward appearance. This combination of personalities was served by comparatively young and alert staff members who were allowed a great latitude of action and independence of thought.

General Ushijima's main battle force was withdrawn to an outpost zone just north of Futema, while elements of the 1st Specially Established Regiment were loosely disposed in the area immediately behind the Hagushi beaches. Although this was the least likely place where they expected the Americans to land, the Japanese troops defending this area were to fight a delaying action in any such eventuality, and then, after destroying the Yontan and Kadena airfields, were to beat a hasty retreat to the Shuri lines.

In the suspected invasion area, the Minatoga beaches, the bulk of the Japanese infantry and artillery forces were positioned to oppose the landings. It was the 2nd Marine Division's assignment to hold them there. And, they would do just that.

SECOND DIVISION "DEMONSTRATION"

In military terminology, a demonstration is a false attack or show of force on a front made with the aim of deceiving the enemy. A related diversionary maneuver, the feint, involves actual contact with the enemy, unlike a demonstration. Admiral Turner had recommended a feint on the southeastern beaches of Okinawa in the initial plan for Operation ICEBERG and that's what actually took place.

Optimum weather conditions for an amphibious landing prevailed at the target on L-Day when the Central Pacific Task Forces launched the attack against Okinawa on 1 April 1945, Easter Sunday. The coming of dawn revealed cloudy to clear skies and a calm sea with but a negligible surf at the shore. Moderate easterly to northeasterly winds were blowing offshore, just enough to carry the smoke away from the beaches. To the many veteran jungle fighters among the invading troops, the 75-degree temperature seemed comfortably cool. At the target, the major naval lift and support elements moved into their assigned areas off the Hagushi beaches. Once in position, the ships prepared to disembark their troops. Off the Minatoga beaches on the other side of the island, the same preparations were

SECOND DIVISION "DEMONSTRATION"

conducted concurrently by the shipping that carried the 2nd Marine Division in order to carry out the Demonstration.

During the period of prelanding preparation, the Japanese 32nd Army had been able to keep its tactical dispositions well concealed. Although the American planners knew generally where the enemy was disposed, actual revelation of many Japanese positions would await the probing attacks of ground elements. Overbalancing this enemy achievement was the American success in maintaining the illusion of a landing on the Minatoga beaches on the southeast tip of Okinawa. Naval bombardment and Underwater Demolition Team (UDT) operations had convinced the enemy staff that "the possibility could not be ruled out, that powerful elements might attempt a landing." Accordingly, a substantial portion of the enemy's artillery and infantry strength would be kept out of the first days' action by the feint landing of the Second Division. But there was a cost to be paid by the Silent Second.

Operation ICEBERG got off to a roaring start. The few Japanese still in the vicinity of the main assault at first light on L-Day, 1 April 1945, could immediately sense the wisdom of General Ushijima in conceding the landing to the Americans. The enormous armada, assembled from ports all over the Pacific Ocean, had concentrated on schedule off Okinawa's southwest coast and stood coiled to project its 182,000-man landing force over the beach.

Admiral Turner made his final review of weather conditions in the amphibious objective area. As at Iwo Jima, the amphibians would be blessed with good weather on the critical first day of the landing. Skies would be cloudy to clear, winds moderate east to northeast, surf moderate, temperature 75 degrees. Admiral Turner unleashed his forces at 0406 with the traditional order, "Land the Landing Force," and Okinawa's ordeal began with a percussive overture of naval gunfire. The enemy reacted to the landing shortly after dawn as he mounted scattered air attacks on the convoys. Combat troops already manning the rails of their transports witnessed an unforgettable display of naval power--the sustained bombardment by shells and rockets from hundreds of ships, alternating with formations of attack aircraft streaking low over the beaches, bombing and strafing at will. Enemy return fire seemed scattered and ineffectual, even against such a mass of lucrative targets assembled offshore. Turner confirmed H-Hour at 0830.

Now came the turn of the 2nd Marine Division and the ships of the Diversionary Force to decoy the Japanese with a feint landing on the opposite coast. The amphibious force

SECOND DIVISION "DEMONSTRATION"

steamed into position, launched amphibian tractors and Higgins boats, loaded them conspicuously with combat-equipped Marines, then dispatched them towards Minatoga Beach in seven waves.

USS Sibley (APA 206)
Source http://www.navsource.org/archives/10/03/03206.htm

Marines load the landing craft at Okinawa 1 April 1945

Coast Guard manned LST off loads Marines and Amphibious tractors

THE SILENT SECOND

Paying careful attention to the clock, the fourth wave commander crossed the line of departure exactly at 0830, the time of the real H-Hour for the 1st and 6th Marines and the Army to land on the west coast. The 2nd Division's LVTs and boats then turned sharply away and returned to the transports, mission accomplished. In the continuing belief that the main effort was directed at the Minatoga area, the few Japanese aircraft not destroyed by American carrier air or ships' antiaircraft guns disregarded the more lucrative targets off Hagushi and concentrated on Demonstration Group shipping.

Battleship fires on Kamikaze at Okinawa-1 April 1945

SECOND DIVISION "DEMONSTRATION"

When the 2nd Marine Division made its feint landings on L-Day and L plus 1, the Japanese commander's staff believed its earlier estimate that "powerful elements might attempt a landing [on the Minatoga beaches]" was fully justified. Consequently, a substantial portion of the artillery and infantry strength of the Japanese Thirty-second Army was immobilized in face of a threat to the beaches on the southeast that would prove to be a successful feint, just as Admiral Turner envisaged.

Amphibious approach to Okinawa 1 April

Okinawa Landing L-day 1 April 1945

Marine Amtracs on Okinawa western beachhead

THE SILENT SECOND

Although Ushijima's command had prepared for an American landing elsewhere, from the Japanese soldier's point of view the Hagushi beaches remained the most obvious target because of their close proximity to the airfields. Even while propaganda reports—mostly untrue—of successful Kamikaze attacks against the invasion fleet bolstered Japanese morale, the commander of a scratch force formed from airfield personnel on the island warned his men not "to draw the hasty conclusion that we had been able to destroy the enemy's plan of landing on Okinawa Jima."

But the Silent Second was hit. Japanese kamikaze pilots were convinced that that the multiple waves of landing craft off the Minatoga beaches were part of the main landing. They struck the Demonstration force, seriously damaging the troopship Hinsdale and LST 844. The 3rd Battalion, 2nd Marines, and the 2nd Amphibian Tractor Battalion suffered nearly 50 casualties; the two ships lost an equal number of sailors and coast guard. Ironically, the division expected to have the least damage or casualties in the L-Day battle lost more men than any other division in the Tenth Army that day. Complained division Operations Officer Lieutenant

Colonel Samuel G. Taxis: "We had asked for air cover for the feint but were told the threat would be 'incidental.'"

USS Hinsdale (APA-120)
Source- military.wikia.com/wiki/USS_Hinsdale_(APA-120)

USS Hinsdale Action Report

As the Hinsdale steamed toward the transport area through the pre-dawn blackness, Marines already on deck and ready to disembark, Hinsdale's lookouts spotted an enemy plane skimming low over the water.

With only a few seconds warning, Hinsdale could not evade the Kamikaze; at 0600 the suicide plane crashed into her port side just above the water line and ripped into the engine room. Three explosions rocked the troop-laden transport as the kamikaze's bombs exploded deep inside her and tore the engine room apart— only one member of the watch survived death by scalding steam from the exploding boilers.

The deck-log of the Hinsdale has the following account: "0549 in a position about 12 miles south-southeast of the southern tip of Okinawa the ship was hit amidships on the port side and two explosions at intervals of about one second were felt. Later investigation indicated that a Japanese suicide plane, probably a Tony Kawasaki Ki-61 carrying three 132 lb. bombs hit the ship on the port side at the water line in the vicinity of frame 80. The ship was holed in three places: A seven foot hole in the engine room at the water line caused by the engine and fuselage to which it is believed was attached a bomb which was the first explosion, a ten inch hole in the engine room about 2 feet above the water line caused by a bomb which was later discovered as a dud, and a four foot hole in Compartment A-304-EL a crew's berthing space, caused by a bomb which was the second explosion."

Power failed immediately—lights and internal communication, so vital to damage control parties, were gone. Hinsdale came to a dead stop in the water, with three gaping holes in her port side. Marines on deck who had been ready to disembark were hastily shifted to the starboard rails to counteract a serious list to port. Below

SECOND DIVISION "DEMONSTRATION"

decks Hinsdale's crew were groping through the smoke-filled darkness to fight fires started by the Kamikaze and to jury-rig patches. Fifteen men were dead; 40 missing or wounded. Despite the injury Hinsdale carried out her job to put the Marines ashore. There were many un-sung heroes that morning one of whom was First Class Metalsmith James O. Perry. Petty Officer Perry saw the Kamikaze plane approaching and cleared the topside of Marines and Sailors thus saving many lives.

Kamikazi damage to USS Hinsdale

LST 884 Action Report

LST 884 was one of a group of invasion vessels also selected to make the diversionary feint on the southern beaches of Okinawa. With a force of Marines and a cargo that included ammunition as well as amphibious combat vehicles, LST 884 had made the run from Saipan to the assault area without incident.

"At 04:00 in the morning on L-day the Marines were alerted and all hands stood by to carry out the assault schedule. At 05:21, three Japanese planes were sighted by the gun crews of the 884 and other ships in the convoy. They all opened fire on the incoming aircraft. Two of the planes were shot down without damage to shipping. The third, making a suicide attempt, hit the 884. Although the pilot was dead, the plane went into a shallow dive and smashed into the Coast Guard ship just above the waterline and just aft of the forward part of the superstructure. The plane, in flames when it hit, drove into the 884 with a terrific impact that carried it through a sleeping compartment, thrusting its forward portion through a second bulkhead and on down through the shipfitter's shop to eventually halt on the tank deck.

As repair parties raced to the scene fire broke out in the main engine room which was brought under control in a short time. But the crash had started a fire on the tank deck and also the ammunition cargo which it carried.

As this explosive load started to detonate the situation was made doubly perilous by fire which swept the amphibious tractors on the tank deck which were ready for debarkation. Clouds of yellow acrid smoke increased the hazards of fire, buckling bulkheads, from explosions and one of the two bombs carried by the suicide plane was wedged in the engine room escape hatch and burning. The crew did not know until later that this was potential death in the form of an unexploded 250-pound bomb. It did not go off, however, but remained where it had lodged and during the days that followed was a very real threat.

Due to the situation on the tank deck it was impossible to enter the tank deck and fire lines were dropped down vents in an effort to limit the fire. The crash had knocked out of commission several water lines, and in both the main and auxiliary engine rooms the situation was rapidly becoming untenable as smoke and heat made it impossible for the men there to continue fire-fighting. Fumes from the fuel tanks increased the hazard and the ship was rocked repeatedly by violent explosions. Limited space already congested by 300 additional personnel, the Marine units, forbade easy movement of the fire fighters and Lt. C.C. Pearson of St. Petersburg, FL, the commanding officer, passed word for all hands to stand by to abandon ship.

Just before this word was passed one of the ship's small boats had been lowered to pick up two men knocked off a nearby LST by an unidentified explosion. These men were rescued, the boat then stood by to pick up personnel from its own ship. The port boat was lowered, life rafts released, and the crew left the ship after destroying confidential records and equipment. Men in the water were picked up by their own boats and those from nearby ships. Lieutenant Pearson then left the ship and was taken aboard a destroyer which was standing by. The entire sequence, from the time the guns first opened on the attacking planes until Pearson had passed the word had taken less than half an hour. Other ships in the unit approached the 884 and attempted to play streams on the fire but at that time they were un-successful. About an hour after leaving his ship, Pearson decided that the heavier portion of the ammunition had been exploded and it might be possible to get the fires under control. He requested permission from the commodore of the group to return to the 884 with a volunteer party. This was granted and a few minutes later a survey group composed of the Lt. Pearson and his executive officer, Lt. R.B. Day of Long Island, NY, the navigation officer, Lt. S.R. Geist of New York City, Lt. L.B. Frye of Wisconsin (the engineering officer) along with two enlisted men and a Marine officer went to work.

SECOND DIVISION "DEMONSTRATION"

A fire main pump was started by Lt. Day and two streams of water were brought to bear on the fire. At 8:00 additional fire fighters came aboard led by Lt. H.B. Baker of Narragansett, RI, the ship's first lieutenant. Two more Marine officers came with this party which consisted of 15 enlisted men from ship's company.

Numerous ships were standing by at this point and several streams of water were being played on the deck which made it possible for the fire party to move about. At one point, hoses had to be kept on Lt. Pearson and Lt. Geist as they passed flaming hatches.

During the following several hours the fire-fighters fought the blaze which had swept through the after portion of the tank deck, run through the crew's quarters on the portside and completely gutted the captain's and officers' cabins, wardroom and ship's office. The galley had also been razed and a good portion of the starboard living quarters was ruined. Both the main and auxiliary engine rooms had been flooded with water. Electric power was out and along the galley passageway 20mm gun magazines racked up there had been set off. In general, the ship was completely out of action and lay a helpless hull. However, as the fire was brought under control and finally extinguished, salvage parties from the 884 crew as well as from nearby ships assisting in the operation came aboard to restore some sort of order. Although no fatalities had occurred in ship's company it was a number of days before a complete count could be taken as the crew was scattered about among various ships in the area. A number of 2nd Division Marines had been killed in the initial blast and as the day wore on their bodies were removed.

Damage to LST 884 after Kamikaze attack on 1 April 1945

With the fire hazard checked the ship was taken in tow to Karema Retto harbor, an anchorage in a small group of islands just off the southwest coast of Okinawa. This 18-mile journey was completed without incident and once arrived at the anchorage salvage work continued. The days spent at Karema Retto were filled with air alerts and the weary men of the 884 moved about their ghost ship bringing order out of chaos, their work constantly interrupted by air attacks and snipers from the shore.

The one fatality among the crew occurred on the night of April 1 when F.D. Flockencier, Motor Machinist's Mate 1/c, was shot through the neck and killed while standing a security watch on the foredeck of the LST. Coast Guardsmen and Marines went ashore in armed burial parties and the dead now rest on the green and brown slopes of the hilly islands that are Karema Retto."

RETURN TO SAIPAN

For two days, the Marines on the USS Sibley participated in the Demonstration by conducting another feint towards the southeastern beaches and then the task group retired to a waiting area south of the island. On 11 April, Sibley was ordered to return to Saipan, where she unloaded her troops and cargo, but remained on call for possible use in the Okinawa operation until 4 June. All 2nd Marine Division forces were withdrawn from Okinawa with the exception of the 8th Marines.

As April dragged into May, the Tenth Army became bogged down conducting ineffective frontal attacks along the Shuri line. Admirals Spruance and Turner began to press General Buckner to accelerate his tactics in order to decrease the vulnerability of the fleet. Admiral Nimitz, quite concerned, even flew to Okinawa to counsel Buckner. "I'm losing a ship and a half each day out here," Nimitz said, "You've got to get this thing moving."

The senior Marines urged Buckner to "play the amphib card," to execute a major landing on the southeast coast, preferably along the alternate beaches at Minatoga, in order to turn the Japanese right flank. They were joined in this recommendation by several Army generals who already perceived what a meatgrinder the frontal assaults along the Shuri line were beginning to become. The Commandant of the Marine Corps, General Alexander A. Vandegrift, visited the island and seconded these suggestions to Buckner. After all, Buckner still had control of the 2nd Marine Division, a veteran amphibious outfit which had demonstrated effectively against the Minatoga Beaches on L-Day. Buckner had subsequently returned the embarked division to Saipan to reduce its vulnerability to additional kamikaze attacks, but the unit still had its assigned ships at hand, still combat loaded. The 2nd Marine Division could have opened a second front in Okinawa within a few days.

While General Buckner was a popular, competent commander, he had limited experience with amphibious warfare and possessed a conservative nature. His staff warned of logistics problems involved in a second front. His intelligence advisors predicted stiff enemy resistance around the Minatoga beachhead. Buckner had also heard enough of the costly Anzio operation in Italy to be leery of any landing executed too far from the main effort. He honestly believed the Japanese manning the Shuri defenses would soon crack under the synchronized application of all his massed firepower and infantry. Buckner therefore rejected the amphibious option out of hand. Surprisingly, Nimitz and his Chief of Staff, Rear Admiral Forrest Sherman, agreed.

THE SILENT SECOND

Not so Admirals Spruance and Turner or the Marines. As Spruance later admitted in a private letter, "There are times when I got impatient for some of Holland Smith's drive." General Shepherd noted, "General Buckner did not cotton to amphibious operations." Even Colonel Hiromichi Yahara, Operations Officer of the Thirty-second Army, admitted under interrogation that he had been baffled by the American's adherence to a purely frontal assault from north to south. "The absence of a landing [in the south] puzzled the Thirty-second Army staff," he said, "particularly after the beginning of May when it became impossible to put up more than a token resistance in the south."

By then the 2nd Marine Division was beginning to feel like a yo-yo in preparing for its variously assigned missions for Operation ICEBERG. Lieutenant Colonel Taxis, Division G-3, remained unforgiving of Buckner's decision. "I will always feel," he stated after the war, "that the Tenth Army should have been prepared the instant they found they were bogged down, they should have thrown a left hook down there in the southern beaches . . . . They had a hell of a powerful reinforced division (The 2nd Division), trained to a gnat's whisker."

Buckner stood by his decision. There would be no "left hook." Instead, both the 1st and the 6th Marine Divisions would join the Shuri offensive as infantry divisions under the Tenth Army. The 2nd Marine Division, less one reinforced regimental landing team (the 8th Marines), would languish back in Saipan.

The post-L-Day amphibious operations of the 77th and 27th Divisions and the FMF-Pacific Force Recon Battalion were professionally executed and beneficial, but not decisive. By mid-April, the Tenth Army had decided to wage a campaign of massive firepower and attrition against the main Japanese defenses. General Buckner chose not to employ his many amphibious resources to break the ensuing gridlock.

Buckner's consideration of the amphibious option was not helped by a lack of flexibility on the part of the Joint Chiefs of Staff who kept strings attached to the Marine divisions. The Thirty-second Army in southern Okinawa clearly represented the enemy center of gravity in the Ryukyu Islands, but the JCS let weeks lapse before scrubbing earlier commitments for the 2nd Marine Division to assault Kikai Shima, an obscure island north of Okinawa, and the 1st and 6th Marine Divisions to tackle Miyako Shima, near Formosa. Of the Miyako Shima mission Lieutenant

THE SILENT SECOND

General Holland M. Smith observed, "It is unnecessary, practically in a rear area, and its capture will cost more than Iwo Jima." General Smith no longer served in an operational capacity, but his assessment of amphibious plans still carried weight. The JCS finally canceled both operations, and General Buckner had unrestricted use of his Marines on Okinawa. By then he had decided to employ them in the same fashion as his Army divisions.

Generals Shepard and Buckner on Okinawa

Buckner did avail himself of the 8th Marines from the 2nd Marine Division, employing it first in a pair of amphibious landings during 3-9 June to seize outlying islands for early warning radar facilities and fighter direction centers against kamikaze raids. The commanding general then attached the reinforced regiment to the 1st Marine Division for the final overland assaults in the south. The 2nd Marine Division's 8th Marine Regiment took part in several landings on islands elsewhere in the Ryukyus in late May, then went ashore on Okinawa to fill out the 1st Marine Division for the final assaults of the campaign.

On 18 June 1945, General Buckner was killed by a Japanese artillery shell in the 8th Marines line while reconnoitering the front. The next senior general officer on the scene was Marine Maj. Gen. Roy Geiger, the IIIAC commanding general. Geiger, an aviator who had commanded the 1st Marine Aircraft Wing at Guadalcanal, 1st Marine Amphibious Corps at Bougainville and IIIAC at Guam and Okinawa, was spot-promoted to lieutenant general to become the first and only Marine and the first and only naval aviator — perhaps the first and only aviator — ever to command an American army in the field.

General Geiger and his operations planners at Okinawa

General Roy Geiger

It is also ironic that the Second Marine Division and other units involved in the Demonstration, not even scheduled to land on Okinawa on L-Day, sustained the first troop casualties of this major and final Pacific battle of World War II. Over thirty Marines in the Second Division joined by their comrades in the Coast Guard gave their lives for their Country on that fateful day. It's a story that needs to be remembered and is one of the main reasons for this book.

POST WORLD WAR II

It is hard to be a Marine officer in peacetime. The assignments are routine and administrative. My dad had duty assignments that included being the OIC of the Fifth Area Post Exchange and Service Club at Camp Lejeune. In the 1947 to 1949 timeframe, the Capages family was relocated to the base at Camp Lejeune. In 1948 my dad was away for an extended period of time on maneuvers in Guam and near Puerto Rico.

In February 1948, Captain Capages boarded the USS Okanogan (APA 220) in Morehead City NC and headed for Vieques. At the time he was the Communications Officer for the 1st Provisional Artillery Battalion. During February-March, all of the major elements of the division participated in a major training mission (FLEX-'48) in conjunction with the largest (up to then) Atlantic Fleet maneuvers (Operation Bouncer) at Vieques. During that time on Vieques, there were continuous training and field exercises utilizing all of the principles involving infantry units in the attack. This included many night problems as well as combined arms exercises. While it had participated in the early phase of FLEX-'48 (code name for the Vieques operation), the 8th Marines detached from the exercises and proceeded to the

Mediterranean where it relieved the 2nd Marines which was then deployed with the 6th Fleet. (Banning, 1988)

By the summer of 1948 the Marine Corps had shrunk to a postwar low in manpower of 85,000. The steady attrition process was keenly felt in the 2nd Division where two-year men were departing daily, many for early separation. Because of the shortfall in personnel, many of the so-called unit deployments included men borrowed from other commands.

Things started off in high gear as the Second Division ushered in the new year, 1949. On 3 January, the 2nd Marines deployed for its second "Med." cruise, there to relieve the 4th Marines. For most of the other units, the weeks were spent in routine training exercises in preparation for FLEX '49, still another major Atlantic Fleet (and FMF) amphibious operation.

On 9 February the following division units (most of them badly understrength) left for Vieques: 1st Provisional Regiment (less 2nd Marines), the 2nd Provisional Regiment, the 10th Marines (or what constituted that proud unit at the time) and the division's remaining organic units. Captain Capages was in the 1st Battalion, 10th Marines. The force arrived at Vieques on 2 March. That year's maneuvers were to have some new wrinkles, not the least of which was the presence of Army "aggressor forces." The "aggressors" did their job of defending their perimeter with determination and enthusiasm.

Dressed in distinctive uniforms, the Army used skillful tactics to provide a special dimension of realism to the exercises. On one occasion, aggressor forces set fire to a hillside, thus forcing the Marines (then occupying a defensive position) to relocate and revise their maneuver strategy. In late 1949, Captain Capages was transferred to the 1st Provisional Artillery Battalion, 11th Marines at Camp Pendleton.

THE HOME FRONT

Camp Lejeune and Camp Pendleton 1946-49

I already mentioned my earliest memory of receiving my small pox shot at Camp Lejeune. Another memory is when we were living on the base in married officer's quarters. The quarters were two story homes and at age 4-1/2, I managed to lock myself in the upstairs bathroom. I panicked and couldn't unlock the door. Dad was away on maneuvers as usual. I remember that a man who lived next door came over, put up a ladder and entered through the bathroom window. He then just flipped the latch on the door from the inside. Later on, my mom would tell me that the man was a Marine Lieutenant Colonel. Semper Fi, Sir. At this time we had a family dog. A large male Doberman name Tripoli. Dad loved Dobermans. It's a Marine thing. There would be more Capages Tripoli's.

In late 1949 Dad was transferred to Camp Pendleton and I was enrolled in kindergarten. My sister, Candace "Candy" was two-years-old and my youngest sister, Cheryl "Chery" was just a year old. Candy was born at Camp Lejeune and Chery was born at the Naval Air Station hospital in Millington. Mom had her hands full. We left the wonderful two-story home on beautiful Camp Lejeune and moved into a Quonset hut on the base that we shared with another Marine family. The family members were Native Americans. It is possible that they were Navajo and the head of the family, was perhaps a "code talker". This is conjecture but makes sense since Dad was an artillery officer and forward observer in a signal battalion. My dad and his Navajo comrade were very close. Dad was an avid archer and loved to design bows and special arrows. Dad's friend showed him how to make a traditional Navajo quiver for his arrows. He kept it for most of his life. He had a deep, abiding love for the Navajos and all Native Americans. This may have been the reason he encouraged my cousin, Peggy, to go to Oklahoma and teach the Native American children there.

After a few months, we moved to a more traditional residence in Oceanside, California which may have been off of the base. I just recall that it was a home that backed up to a deep canyon. One time, Dad took me hunting down in the bottom of that canyon. I had a little bow with arrows with field points. We walked with one arrow notched on the bowstring. Dad walked ahead of me, showing me how to put the ball of my foot down quietly, then transferring my weight to the heel. I was paying too much attention to this quiet walking business and didn't noticed when Dad stopped. I walked right into him and one of my arrows stuck him in the rear. He would tell that story for years. I also remember getting lost for the first time, not in the canyon, but in the residential area. All the homes were identical and I couldn't find mine. I panicked but it was short lived. I was standing in my own driveway. Officer material in the making.

Great Lakes and Winthrop Harbor

Dad was elated when he got the opportunity to get further into military electronics and communications at Great Lakes in July 1950. The family was able to go with him. We moved into a little house in Winthrop Harbor and learned about snow and cold weather. I was six and in the first grade. You know the old story, we "walked through snow drifts 5 ft. high to get to school." Baloney of course. When my best friend Doug and I would get home, we were always soaking wet. My mother followed us home one day just to find out what was going on. She watched as Doug and I plowed through every snow drift we could find, then lay down in the snow making snow angels. This was followed by spirited snow ball fights with other kids along the way home. Winter began in later September with snow, then ice. I learned to ice skate on the gravel road in front of the house. The gravel had 4 inches of packed snow with ice on top. It was perfect.

KOREA

Television was new in 1951. We got our first television set and Dad spent hours getting the picture just right. It was Howdy Doody time and Tom Corbett, Space Cadet. But, Straight Arrow was still big on the radio. In those days you could save cereal box tops and send off for some special gift. I saved up and sent off for a Straight Arrow miniature flash light. It took 6 weeks to arrive. I drove my mom crazy waiting for the darn thing. Spring came late then it was back to hot and humid Millington, Tennessee. My dad had finished the course at Great Lakes in July 1951 and was assigned to the First Marine Division, The Old Breed, headed for Korea where he would command a Radio Relay platoon in the First Signal Battalion.

KOREA

At the end of World War II, the Allies agreed to establish a four-power trusteeship for the peninsula nation of Korea, which, until that time, had been under the control of Japan. This decision, reached at the Yalta conference in 1945, resulted in the establishment of two different Korean governments: The Republic of Korea (ROK), the democratic nation of South Korea, and the Democratic People's Republic of Korea, Communist North Korea. The 38th parallel was defined as the boundary between the two nations. By early 1949 North Korea had obtained a massive amount of weaponry from the Soviet Union and Communist China and was poised to invade the non-Communist south.

Although Cold War tensions between the United States and the Soviet Union were increasing, the Truman administration did not anticipate another major military conflict any time soon after the end of World War II. For that reason, the administration's policy was to downsize the military from 1945 to 1950. In a January 1950 policy statement, U.S. Secretary of State Dean Acheson declared that Korea was outside the United States line of defense. This statement emboldened the North Koreans, who, in the predawn hours of Sunday, 25 June 1950, crossed the 38th parallel into South Korea. Although caught off-guard and unprepared by the invasion, the United States quickly reversed its position and committed forces in support of South Korea. On 26 June President Truman ordered the use of U.S. planes and naval vessels against North Korean forces, and on 30 June U.S. ground troops were deployed. The United Nations Security Council created a United Nations Command (UNC) in support of South Korea, which was the first collective action engaged in by that organization. On the opposite side, Soviet and Chinese troops and pilots helped to bolster the North Korean forces.

General Douglas MacArthur, the senior American commander and soon designated Commander of the UNC, watched the ROK resistance disintegrate and on 2 July 1950 requested a Marine Brigade complete with air support. The 1st Provisional Marine Brigade was consequently formed and departed for the Far East beginning 10 July. At Marine Corps prompting, MacArthur then made three requests for the 1st Marine Division, which would conduct the amphibious masterstroke at the western port town of Inchon on 15 September. This landing and the simultaneous advance of the UNC forces defending the Pusan perimeter shattered the North Korean Army, which effectively ceased to exist south of the Yalu River. At Camp

Lejeune, the 2nd Marine Division, reconstituted after having initially provided a significant amount of the 1st Marine Division's manpower in 1950, remained focused on the Atlantic, Caribbean, and Mediterranean, while also serving as a replacement pool for the Marines in Korea.

In November 1950 the Communist Chinese intervened on behalf of North Korea, and through September 1951 the war was one of mobility, with the belligerents repeatedly seizing and being driven back from large areas on both sides of the 38th parallel. Thereafter the war entered a phase of protracted, positional warfare, in which both sides operated from semi-fixed lines and fortified strong points, akin to the character of World War I warfare. The war became a battle for hills and ridges, which changed hands often, sometimes several times in one day. The battles were close and personal, with the infantry often fighting side-by-side with the artillery, and man-to-man with the enemy.

Military operations in Korea have just recently been declassified. My dad's records over this timeframe that were provided by the National Personnel Records Center were limited in detail. The records show that he had been promoted to Captain and was assigned as a communications officer of a signal company in the 1st Signal Battalion then a platoon commander of a Radio Relay platoon in the 1st Signal Battalion. At this time, the 1st Marine Division was involved with a considerable number of offensive and defensive artillery operations involving battery and counter-battery firing assignments. The 1st Marine Division was occupying, defending and improving positions on the KANSAS line in North Korea. The Division sent out many patrols in order to maintain contact with the enemy forces. The enemy would retaliate with frequent, small night probing attacks while harassing the Division with 120 mm mortar fire and 76 mm artillery fire. Communications between artillery units, air attack units, naval gun crews and Headquarters were critical. Radio communications between artillery units and superior firing solutions was Captain Capages particular area of expertise.

United Nations intervention in Korea, following the Communist aggression of 25 June 1950, found the United States forces in the Far East inadequate both in numbers and training. Initially, indeed, the United States was hard-pressed to maintain a foothold on the Korean peninsula. A bitter struggle of several months ensued before the North Korean invasion was contained, then crushed. The subsequent Chinese Communist invasion won some swift preliminary successes, but it was also contained early in 1951. Known as a "police action" with no formal declaration of war, the Korean War did not end with an accustomed victory, but in a stalemate, with an armistice or cease-fire agreement on 27 July 1953.

THE SILENT SECOND

Korean Hemorrhagic Fever had not been encountered by United States military personnel before the action in Korea in 1951. This was a failure in intelligence gathering. In fact, Headquarters 1st Marine Division FMF Intelligence Study 1-51 issued 7 April 1951 did not list Hemorrhagic Fever as a potential problem. Today, researchers have concluded that the disease was endemic before 1950 and it may have been missed because of lack of knowledge and its rare occurrences in rural areas due to special ecology. In 1951, there were 827 cases in the U. S. Forces. My dad was one of them.

In late September 1951, Captain Capages contracted hemorrhagic fever and was hospitalized in Japan. His weight dropped from 165 lbs. to 110 lbs. His skin turned completely black. The Japanese nurses thought it was strange that the U. S. Marines had an African-American officer. He said the nurses were always peeking in at him and giggling. At the time, the Marines were still in the process of desegregation. President Truman had issued Executive Order No. 9981 on 26 July 1948. The order stated that "It is hereby declared to be the policy of the President that there shall be equality of treatment and opportunity for all persons in the armed services without regard to race, color, religion, or national origin." There was resistance to this order within the military. Full integration did not come until the Korean War was in full swing when heavy casualties forced segregated units to merge for survival.

Captain Capages in Japan-1952

Captain Capages in Japan -January 1952

My dad started to gain his weight back and his skin started to slough off between his fingers and toes. He was finally well enough to be sent to Hawaii on a hospital ship. As the ship entered the harbor, the wounded warriors were welcomed by fire-fighting tug boats spraying water into the air followed by hula girls dancing on main deck of the hospital ship. Dad had purchased an 8 mm camera in Japan and filmed everything he saw, especially the hula girls. He also filmed a carrier anchored next to the hospital ship. It was the USS Valley Forge (CV 45) that was loaded with Naval and Marine Aircraft and ready to raise anchor to head for Korea. The men on the hospital ship were probably glad they were headed the other way.

USS Valley Forge CV45

Operation Crossover-Onslow Beach

Despite ongoing construction and the activity of reorganization, from 1946-1950 Camp Lejeune was quiet relative to its bustling World War II period. Summer reserve training, the semi-annual rotation of a battalion to the Navy's 6th Fleet in the Mediterranean, and occasional exercises continued at the base; however, it wasn't until 21 April 1950 that the first major post-World War II landing exercise, Operation Crossover, occurred at Onslow Beach.

For my dad, it was off to Camp Pendleton followed by a temporary relocation near the family in Millington, Tennessee at the Naval Air Station. He was finally well in late April 1952 and was reassigned to the Second Division at Camp Lejeune.

PEACETIME 1953-56

Back Home-Camp Lejeune

We spent a few weeks on Top Sail Island while Dad commuted to and from the base. The time on Top Sail Island was a bit surreal. We would fish for crabs and boil them for dinner, almost every other day. Mom would have us walk along the beach and pick up sea shells. Dad would come home for the weekend if he wasn't on maneuvers. One time, when he was expected to be away for an extended time, he took me camping on the beach. We set up a pup tent, cut some thick slices of bacon and fried them in a pan over the fire. It was the best thing I ever tasted. Then we tried to sleep. Dad had a watch with radium numbers and hands that I could see in the night. And, I could see his face when he would take a draw on his cigarette. It was very comforting to a seven-year-old. In the morning, he showed me how to clean the frying pan using beach sand. Mom would not have approved. Mom had her own problems. There was no refrigerator in the little beach bungalow, just an icebox. And, ice was hard to come by. We had to evacuate the premises once due to the spoilage of some pork sausage that Mom forgot was in the icebox. I can smell it to this day.

We then moved to New River and stayed in a duplex. Back to civilization. The couple in the next unit were Major Jack "Smiley" Hilburn and his wife Constance "Connie". They would become my dad and mom's best friends. Smiley Hilburn was a Marine Aviator who was highly regarded by everyone who knew him. Connie Hilburn was a star athlete in high school and an avid golfer. She tried to teach me how to swing a baseball bat. "Now Cappy, swing level," she would say. I didn't get the hang of it until the 7th grade. I remember when they adopted their first child. They named her Lindee. I thought she was the cutest little thing I had ever seen. I helped her learn to walk and felt like she was part of our family, another little sister. Smiley was transferred to San Antonio and eventually assigned to the El Toro base in California. After he retired, he would conduct tours of the facility that had been converted to a Naval and Marine aviation museum. Major Hilburn passed away in May 2003. His beautiful wife, Connie, passed away in 2016. They were wonderful people.

I attended the third grade in New River and learned to roller skate on the driveway and the sidewalk around the duplexes. The construction was all new at the time. My third grade teacher was Mrs. Hamola (sp), a wife of a Marine. It was in the 3rd grade that I decided that I didn't like my nickname, Cappy, and decided that henceforth, I would be called Martin. I didn't see a problem with that since Dad went by Marty. I am still Cappy to my sisters and cousins. That will never change, apparently.

In 1954, we were assigned quarters on the base. We lived in a bungalow at 3322 Onslow Drive. This was a fantastic location with a beautiful, landscaped traffic circle just in front of the home. These are perhaps, my happiest memories from the Marines. I attended the 4th Grade in the elementary school on the base. While we had learned to say the pledge of allegiance in the 3rd grade, we now learned to add "under God." It took a while to get the hang of it. Another thing that was a must have item for 4th grade boys was a pair of leather gloves. I don't know why, perhaps we all wanted to be cowboys. Anyway, Mom said it was silly so nothing doing. Then here comes a box from my Aunt Mary Rose. It contained a pair of new leather gloves that were too small for my cousin Jimmy. I didn't care that it was 90 degrees out and the gloves were lined with rabbit fur. I was now up to snuff with my peers.

Mom was the Den Mother of my Cub Scout group and we were always busy. The Marines catered to the Scout groups and would arrange for camp sites, demonstrations of some of the equipment, and would conduct the inspections of the Scouts. It was all "spit and shine". I will never forget one inspection. A Marine major was doing the inspection of each boy's uniform. I thought I was ready and Dad was watching. The Major inspected me and gave a wink at my dad. He held up one finger, then two, and finally three fingers. I had missed three belt loops in the back. My dad was rolling on the floor with laughter. Mission accomplished, never missed a belt loop after that.

As I mentioned earlier, Dad was an avid archery buff. He would read books and articles by Howard Hill and study the history of ancient bows used by the Greeks, Turks and Mongols. He developed many of his own designs and was very intrigued with fiberglass backing for double reflex bows.

When the Marines were home from maneuvers, they partied hard. Mom and Dad would entertain their friends at our house and then the families would get together at someone else's house. There was a lot of alcohol involved in these social events as I recall. I was even instructed in how to prepare a Manhattan at age nine. At one of these parties I remember Dad saying, "A bow with a 150 lb. draw and a broadhead arrow can penetrate further than a bullet from a 1911 Colt 45." One of his officer buddies challenged that statement and the game was on. Dad went home and brought back his bow and a broadhead arrow. They took an olive drab steel bucket and filled it with sand. A service 1911 Colt 45 was loaded with a single round and fired into the bucket. The round penetrated the steel skin of the bucket and flattened out against the sand. It had penetrated about an inch. Then Dad drew back his bow with the broadhead arrow and let fly. The arrow penetrated one side of the steel bucket, went through the sand, and punched through the other side of the bucket. All were amazed. Dad said, "It's just physics." I do not recall any response from the MPs due to the pistol shot. I wouldn't try that today.

North Carolina is noted for the size and number of its mosquitoes. To handle this problem, the Marines would spray DDT in a fine mist all over the base. When the spray truck went by, every kid in the neighbor would run in the mist behind truck. Most of us are still here.

While on the base, my dad bought a new 1949 Hudson Hornet to replace our 1946 Crosley. The Hudson had never been owned and was not painted. It just had gray primer. It had something to do with the shortage of paint following World War II. Dad loved that car and would often brag about it being able to take curves on three wheels if necessary. The car had overdrive, another thing he used to tout about this big, heavy vehicle. He was right of course.

The Hudson Hornet was the queen of the fledgling stock car races and a special favorite of its bootlegger drivers.

Camp Lejeune was special. I got my first 26" bike, a red and black beauty manufactured by Stelber. My best friend, Johnny got a Schwin, a tank model with chrome coil front shocks. I was envious but shouldn't have been. Old Stelber would serve me well for many years. But I didn't know that then. Johnny's bike was beautiful to behold. To make things worse, he would always win our wrestling matches. While about 3 inches shorter than me, he was stocky. He may have outweighed me by 30-40 lbs. Dad took it upon himself to teach me basic Judo moves to include how to disarm someone with a knife. There were other moves that I could hardly wait to try out on my old buddie, Johnny, but then Dad warned me to never use what he taught me unless I was defending my mom or my sisters. What a let-down. But, I would win the marble contests with Johnny using my secret weapon, a steel ball bearing. Remember what my dad said?, "Physics." The apple didn't fall far from that tree.

I remember my first girlfriend. I even remember her name, Beverly Conlin. She was a cute brunette who resembled Darla in the movie "The Lil Rascals". It was a very short romance, after all, we were just fourth graders.

THE SILENT SECOND

We used to play in the landscaped traffic circle in front of the house. The only thing I really remember is going to her birthday party that got cut short when she had an asthma attack. I don't remember her running behind the DDT truck. Maybe she should have.

The inevitable transfer took place once more. This time it was Alameda, California in 1955. We left our beloved Camp Lejeune and headed west. Along the way we visited the Powell family in Millington, Tennessee. It was always the same procedure. When we approached the Powell family driveway, Dad would start honking the horn on the big Hudson Hornet. Nearly all the aunts, uncles and cousins would be there, especially if it was a Sunday. The family would gather around the table to eat fried chicken, black-eyed peas, turnip greens, sweet potatoes, cornbread and home churned butter. My grandfather would always say the same Grace, "Humble our hearts and make us thankful for these and all other blessings." My grandmother would finish her meal and almost always enjoy what she called her "desert". She would crumple up some corn bread and put it in a glass of buttermilk. I never tried it, and I'm glad I didn't. But I may have missed something.

We had to move on towards the West after a great reunion. The next stop was a little town in Missouri called

Branson. It is famous now, but it wasn't in 1954-55. This would turn out to be a big deal in the Capages family history. But you will have to read another book to find out about that.

We drove to California on the southern route across New Mexico and Arizona, then the desert of southeast California. There was no air conditioning in the vehicle. With a great deal of envy, we watched the cars coming by that had evaporative coolers mounted on their side windows. The two-lane asphalt ribbon of highway was never ending. It was up and down like a roller coaster with a mirage that looked like water at every dip in the road. The mirage would always disappear before you got to it. But finally, there were pine trees, mountains and then orange groves. It was California and time to be Marine brats once again.

We moved into temporary quarters on the Almeda Naval Air Station for about 6 weeks then moved to a rental home on Pacific Avenue in Alameda. While there, I attended Washington elementary school in the 5th grade. It was my first and last experience with a bully on the playground. I remember that he poked his finger on my chest three times. On the third poke, I pushed him hard on the chest with both hands and he fell to the ground on his back. He wasn't expecting it, but it didn't matter. His rule of the playground was over. I was a hero but never accepted a crown. It was timely since Mom had enrolled me in a summer church camp where we learned the Ten Commandments and the Golden Rule. The teacher even showed us how make a parchment scroll with the Commandments written in ink then coated with shellac. My mom kept that scroll until our house burned down in the 1980s. The fire also destroyed most of the family photos including the originals of the family's time in the Marines. Some of the photos in this book have been restored from damaged originals or were provided by relatives and family friends.

During 5th grade class time, our teacher had us send a letter to the information office of each state where we were born. My package of information came from Oklahoma. It included a map of the State, an article about its famous resident, Will Rogers, and pictures of Native Americans. So that was Oklahoma. I didn't know at the time that Oklahoma would be calling me again later in life.

Dad was the Officer-in-Charge of the Marine Recruiting Station and was busy, but, he decided we needed a dog, a Doberman of course. Named Tripoli, of course. This time, a beautiful female. She was perfect in every way.

She was mine (according to me). We also added another female to the family, my sister, Krissy, was born. She was supposed to be named Charissa but while Mom was in recovery they asked Dad how to spell her name. He said Karissa of course. There is no C in the Greek alphabet. Krissy was born premature at 3 lbs. 8 oz. That was difficult in 1955 but she made it through with some damage to her eyesight and hearing. She would overcome those difficulties and become an outstanding teacher of children with special needs. I moved up to the Boy Scouts from the Cubbies. For my 10th birthday Dad got me a J.C. Higgins 22 caliber single shot rifle. I was a bit young so, I think Dad got the rifle for himself. But he taught me all of the Marine sniper firing positions. That rifle and I would become good friends later on.

The house in Alameda was too small for the growing family, so Mom and Dad got courageous and bought their first house in San Lorenzo, California. The home had a huge fenced backyard. The fence was essentially a 6 ft. tall concrete block wall. It was the perfect place for Tripoli who could clear a 5 ft. tall fence but was intimidated by the 6 ft. tall monster block wall.

I started the 6th grade at Washington Manor Elementary school. My teacher was Mr. John Forbes, a dedicated teacher who looked like Troy Donahue but was even better looking. This had to be his first teaching gig. He drove an Austin Healey or perhaps, a Triumph, and wore one of those flat racing caps with a buckle in the back. I will never forget his classes. He would read Thor Heyerdahl's *Kon-Tiki* to the class then have us make models of that bamboo raft. This was also the time of the Cold War scare and we had to learn to "duck and cover" under our desks. Mr. Forbes would read science fiction stories to the class. I still remember one that kept me awake for quite a while. It had to do with a woman and her newborn baby stranded in space. That's all I'm going to say about it. I remember another girl friend from Mr. Forbes class. As I recall, her name was Janet Hill. I could be wrong. In any case, I was competing with another guy for her affection. It was Valentine's day and we had both given her a Valentine card. She opened his first and smiled. Then she opened mine. I had included a pretty neck scarf in mine. It was the 'in thing' at the time. It fell out and those watching gasped. I had won the battle for affection. My best friend, Jeff Reposa, turned to my competition and said, "He really got you there!" Janet invited me to be her escort to a square dance and then we went to a school dance called a "sock hop". The most popular dance at the time was called the "Bop". Thanks to my cousins, Ginger and Wanda Powell in Millington, I was up to par.

San Lorenzo was a great place to live. The weather was always sunny but mild. Television was a family event with Walt Disney's Mouseketeers, Spin and Marty, The Hit Parade, Lawrence Welk and of course, Gun Smoke. A 49er jacket was a must-have item for any young boy. I had to sell newspapers to get one but was unsuccessful. Then one just mysteriously appeared. As I mentioned earlier, my best friend at the time was Jeff Reposa. He lived just two houses away from mine. We built a soap box racer of sorts. Actually, Jeff's dad and another neighbor did all the work, but we helped. It was a beautiful vehicle but only as fast as the guy pushing it. That was usually me. Jeff was pretty smart about some things. The first Corvette came out about that time and so did the Ford Thunderbird. In those days, tail fins on automobiles was the "in thing." Some guy in the neighborhood bought a new Thunderbird and customized it by adding tail fins. It was awful looking, but I can still see it in my mind today. You have to understand, customizing cars is a California tradition.

California life was marvelous, but it wasn't going to last. In 1956 the Marines went through a peacetime Reduction-in-Force. Dad resigned from the Corps, sold the house and bought a brand-new Plymouth station wagon. It had a push button controlled, automatic transmission, very new technology. That was my dad, always on the leading edge of technology. Then we packed up and moved to Missouri. That story is continued in my book *OZARK COUNTY HEART: Boyhood Memories of a Dora Missouri Farm*. If you are a Marine or Marine brat, I hope you will read it. There are adventures after the Marine Corps, just Follow Me.

THE SILENT SECOND

MARINE CORPS PHOTOS

PFC Capages

Corporal Capages

Sergeant Capages

Marine Handstand

Off Duty in DC - 1947

PHOTO ALBUMS

PFC Capages-1941

PFC Capages 1941

Corporal Capages-1942

THE SILENT SECOND

MARINE BRAT PHOTO ALBUM

2LT Martin Capages, his wife Helen, and Martin Jr.

Helen Capages with Martin Jr. Fort Sill 1944

Martin Jr. and Tripoli- Camp Lejeune 1946

Candy and Martin Jr. at Camp Lejeune 1948

Martin Jr. Fifth birthday-Camp Lejeune 1949

Marine Brats-Candy and Chery Capages

Winthrop Harbor 1951

Our 1946 Crosley

Our 1949 Hudson at Camp Lejeune 1954

PHOTO ALBUMS

Capages babysitter and Major Hilburn
"Tripping the light fantastic" New River 1953

I dunno Cap. I think it needs more rum.
New River - 1953

Connie Hilburn with Candy and Chery Capages
New River- Christmas 1953

Captain Capages, Martin Jr. and Tripoli II
San Lorenzo CA 1956

Captain Capages and daughter Krissy
San Lorenzo CA 1956

Dad and Tripoli II working out-1956

Martin Jr., Candy, Dad and Chery-Last days as Marine family

THE SILENT SECOND

Capages Family 1956-Civilians

OIC 1LT Martin Capages Jr. and XO 2Lt John Wozniak-Kawakami, Japan

1LT Martin Capages Jr. OIC -Kawakami Ammunition Storage Area-Japan-1968

1Lt Martin Capages Jr. OIC Kamakami Meeting with local Japanese School Kids 1969

PHOTO ALBUMS

Martin Capages nephew, Jeff Smith, working at at Gold's Gym in 1973

Jeff Smith second from right, Arnold second from left Gold's Gym 1973

Tripoli III Houston, Texas- 1975

EPILOGUE

My father passed away to his Heavenly reward in May 1997 at age 78. He had retired as the plant operations manager for the Sears store in the Battlefield Mall in Springfield, Missouri and even at that age, he would still be called back to the store to solve some operational problem, in which he was always successful at correcting. As his body weakened from liver cancer (likely caused by his past case of hemorrhagic fever), we discussed his desired final arrangements. He told me he wanted to be "buried in a pine box." They all say that. He also wanted to be buried in a dark blue suit but with his ribbons on his chest. I nodded in agreement, but I had a different plan in mind.

After Dad passed away, I took his ribbons out of the display case and took them to the Marine Recruiting Station in Springfield. A gunnery sergeant there looked at the ribbons then went back into storage area. He brought out a full dress-blue officer's uniform and pinned Dad's medals on them in proper order. Then he gave me the full uniform including the white dress cover and gloves. I will never forget what he said next, "Sir, the Marines take care of their own." Captain Martin Capages, USMC, was laid to rest in a beautiful pine casket and buried in a full military ceremony

EPILOGUE

at the Springfield National Military Veterans Cemetery. And now, the golden streets of Heaven are guarded by one more United States Marine. Semper Fi.

POSTSCRIPT

In 2011, my wife and I made a trip to the east coast and went to Camp Lejeune. A First Sergeant at the gate sponsored our entry onto the base and we were able to go to the bungalow at 3322 Onslow Drive. A young First Lieutenant, Bob Luiz and his wife, Marie, were the occupants of the residence and graciously invited us in and gave us a tour of the home. It was essentially unchanged. I had movie clips on my laptop from our time at the bungalow and showed them to the Luiz's. I think they enjoyed the little bit of history. I know we did. The traffic circle was still there but, while it was early Spring, there were no signs of any landscaping. That was disappointing. I hope this book will encourage the Marines at Camp Lejeune to restore that little oasis to the way it was in 1954, perhaps dedicated to the heroes of Okinawa.

Martin Jr. at 3322 Onslow Dr. February 2011

Traffic Circle at Intersection Onslow, Jones and Pender

ABOUT THE AUTHOR

Martin Capages, Jr. is a retired professional engineer and technical executive. He is an Army veteran and served as the Officer-in-Charge of the U. S. Army Ammunition Storage Area in Kawakami, Japan from 1968-69.

His technical and management experience includes aircraft design, petroleum exploration and production and structural engineering. He began writing political commentary in 2009 and completed his first book, *The Moral Case for American Freedom*, in July 2017. His writing is from the perspective of a conservative and Constitutional originalist. Dr. Capages was born in 1944, at Fort Sill, Oklahoma, the son of Marine captain, Martin Capages of NYC and Helen Elizabeth Powell Capages of Millington, Tennessee. As a Marine "brat", he attended elementary schools all over the US along with his three younger sisters.

Martin is married to Pamela Kay Capages. They have five children and seven grandchildren. Both Martin and Pamela are active members of their local Baptist church and serve in other state and international Christian ministries.

Other Works by Martin Capages Jr. PhD

Boots to Bogeys to Bronze: The Authorized World War II Biography of 2LT Jack C. Pyatt

The Moral Case for American Freedom

Ozark County Heart: Boyhood Memories of a Dora Missouri Farm

A Wakeful Watch: The Authorized Biography of Charles Lindbergh Armstrong

Heartland Rebellion

WORKS CITED

Alexander, J. H. (n.d.). *THE FINAL CAMPAIGN: Marines in the Victory on Okinawa.* Retrieved from www.ibiblio.org: www.ibiblio.org/hyperwar/USMC/USMC-C-Okinawa/index.html

Banning, W. (1988). *Second Marine Division Commemorative Anthology 1940-1949.* Paducah KY: Turner Publishing Company.

Barker, H. (n.d.). *1ST MARINE DIVISION - INTELLIGENCE STUDY HEADQUARTERS FMF - 7.* Retrieved from The Korean War Project.

Barker, H. (n.d.). *1st Marine Division-HIstorical Diary -August 1951.* Retrieved from Korean War Project: htttp://www.koreanwar.org

Bolton, J. C. (n.d.). Retrieved from lst884.org/material/Docs/Article01/Column 01.pdf

Edwin Howard Simmons-The Marine Corps Heritage Foundation. (1998). *The MARINES.* New York NY: Barnes and Noble, Inc.

Frank, B. M. (1968). *Victory and Occupation-History of US Marine Corps Operations in World War II Vol. V.* Washington DC: HIstorical Branch, G-3 Division, Headquaters, U. S. Marine Corps.

Garand, G. W. (1971). *Western Pacific Operations-History of US Marine Corps in WWII Vol. IV.* Washington DC: Historical Division, Headquarters, U. S. Marine Corps.

Gow, I. (1985). *Okinawa 1945-Gateway to Japan.* Garden City NY: Doubleday & Company, Inc.

Guisti, E. H. (1951). *Mobilization of the Marine Corps Rerserve in the Korean Conflict, 1950-51.* Washington DC: HIstorical Branch, G-3 Division, Headquarters United States Marines.

MARINE CORPS BASE CAMP LEJEUNE DURING THE KOREAN WAR. (n.d.). Retrieved from https://www.lejeune.marines.mil/Portals/27/Documents/EMD/Cultural-Resources/Semper%20Fidelis%20Popular%20History%20Publication/11_Chapter%205.pdf

Yahara, H. (1995). *The Battle for Okinawa.* New York, NY: John Wiley & Sons, Inc.

THE SILENT SECOND

INDEX

6th Signal Company, xii
8th Marine, 66

A
Alameda, xii
Arnold Schwarzenegge, 9

B
Buckner, 22, 25, 32, 35, 61, 62, 63, 64, 66

C
Camp Lejeune, xiii, 29, 69, 73, 78, 83, 85, 90, 91, 107
Camp Pendleton, xiv, 6, 17, 29, 71, 73, 83

D
del Valle, 25, 30
Demonstration, 36, 46, 49, 51, 61, 67

F
Fifth Amphibious Corps (VAC), 30
FLEX-'48, 69
floating Reserve, 25
Fort Sill, 6, 16, 17, 109

G
Geiger, 25, 27, 66
Great Lakes, xiv, 75

H
Hagushi Beaches, 24
Hilburn, 86
Hinsdale, 51, 52, 53
Hunt, 17

I
Iwo Jima, xi, 3, 6, 7, 20, 25, 30, 47, 65

J
Jeff Smith, 9

K
Kamikaze, 2, 51, 52, 54
Keise Shima, 25
Kerama Retto, 25
Korea, xi, xiv, 76, 77, 78, 79, 80, 82
Korean Hemorrhagic Fever, 80

L
L-Day, 23, 26, 36, 45, 46, 50, 51, 62, 64, 67
LST 844, 51

M
Millington, xiv, 11, 73, 76, 83, 91, 96, 109
Minatoga Beaches, 24, 62
Missouri, ii

N
Nimitz, 6, 22, 61, 62

O
Okinawa, xi, xiii, xv, 1, 2, 3, 5, 6, 18, 19, 23, 24, 26, 31, 32, 33, 36, 37, 39, 41, 45, 46, 47, 51, 53, 54, 59, 61, 62, 64, 66, 67
Operation Iceberg, xv, 1

113

P

Pearl Harbor, 6, 17
Powell, 11, 12, 32, 33, 91, 96, 109

R

Radio Relay, 76, 79
Reduction in Force, xi

S

Saipan, 6, 17, 29, 30, 31, 32, 33, 35, 55, 61, 62, 64
Schmidt, 30
Shepherd, 29, 63
Silent Second, xi
Smith, 26, 30, 35, 63, 65
Springfield, ii
Spruance, 61, 63

T

The Old Breed, xi
Third Amphibious Corps (IIIAC), 30
Tripoli, 73, 93, 94
Turner, 23, 24, 25, 45, 47, 50, 61, 63

U

U. S. Marine Corps Operations, Volume V in 1968, xiii
USS Sibley (APA-206), 35

V

Vieques, 69, 70

W

Wallace M. Greene Jr., xiii
Watson, 26, 30

Y

Yahara, 41, 63

THE SILENT SECOND

www.ingramcontent.com/pod-product-compliance
Lightning Source LLC
LaVergne TN
LVHW091556060526
838200LV00036B/857